FLASH FORWARD MATH

Written by **Kerrie Baldwin**

Illustrations by **Dave Garbot**

Flash Kids
A Division of Barnes & Noble
122 Fifth Ave
New York, NY 10011

ISBN: 978-1-4114-0638-4

Please submit all inquiries to FlashKids@bn.com

Printed and bound in Canada

Lot #:
11 13 15 16 14 12
03/13

Dear Parent,

Math can be one of the most difficult subjects for young learners. Your child may not fully grasp early concepts such as addition, subtraction, and regrouping—even with a great math teacher and a thorough math textbook. Here to help at home are almost 100 pages of short drills and fun games that will reinforce all math skills taught in the second grade.

This colorful workbook focuses on your child's competence in counting, comparing, adding, and subtracting numbers to 1,000, engaging him or her with coloring, drawing, matching, riddles, mazes, hidden pictures, and simple word problems. Also covered are very basic multiplication and division, simple fractions, tables and graphs, time, money, plane and solid shapes, measurement in inches and centimeters, and patterns.

The activities are designed for your child to handle alone, but you can read along and help with any troublesome concepts. Together you can check answers at the back of the workbook, and you should always give praise and encouragement for his or her effort. In addition, try to find ways to show your child how these number skills apply to everyday situations. For example, ask him or her to count, add, or subtract simple household objects, such as crayons or magnets; make a bar graph to show how many hours are devoted to homework each day of the week; identify and count shapes spotted during a car trip or walk around the neighborhood; or determine the correct coins needed to buy an item at a store. Use your imagination!

Sports Match

Count the balls in each group. Draw a line from the group to its matching numeral.

1.

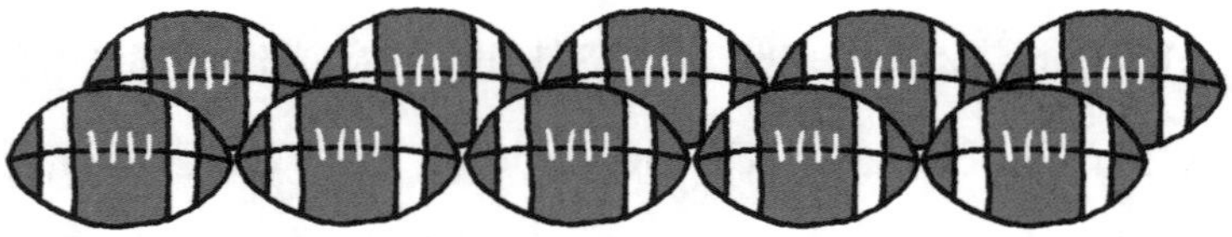

2.

3.

4.

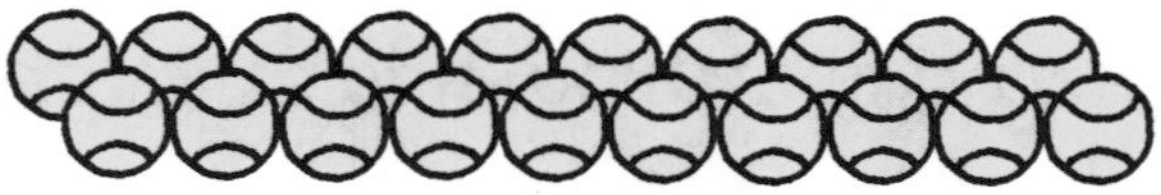

5.

6.

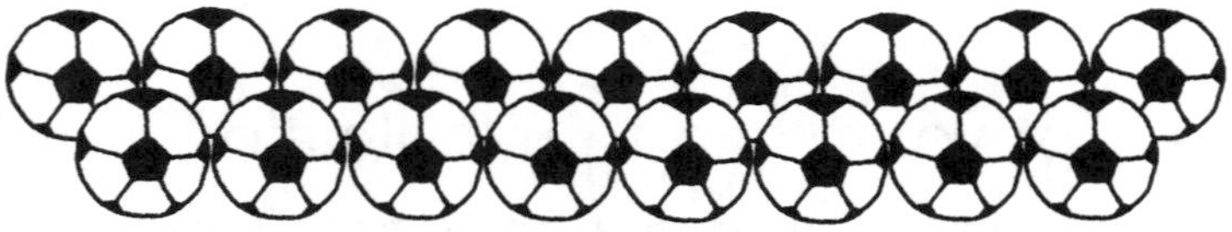

7.

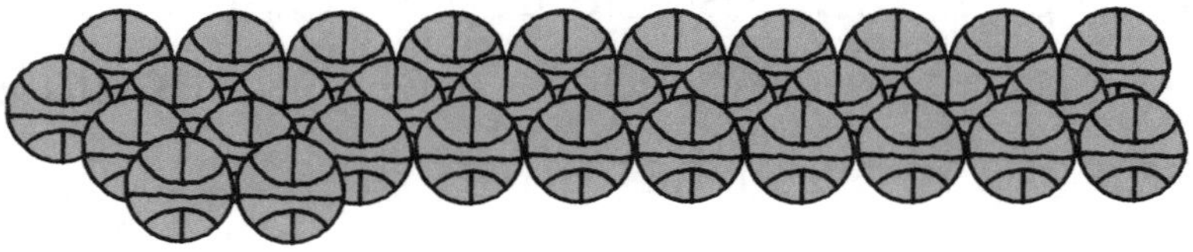

8.

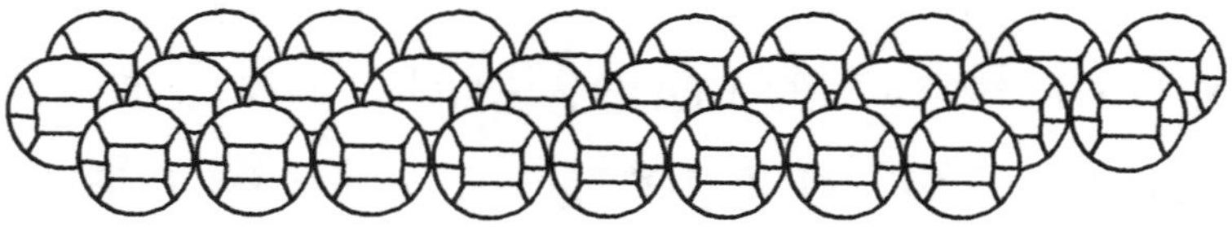

9.

10.

10

17

20

23

28

32

35

39

41

46

Tying Up Tens

Circle groups of ten. Write how many tens and ones.

	Tens	Ones
1.	_____	_____
2.	_____	_____
3.	_____	_____
4.	_____	_____
5.	_____	_____
6.	_____	_____
7.	_____	_____
8.	_____	_____
9.	_____	_____
10.	_____	_____

Skip and Soar

Skip count by 10s to connect the dots.

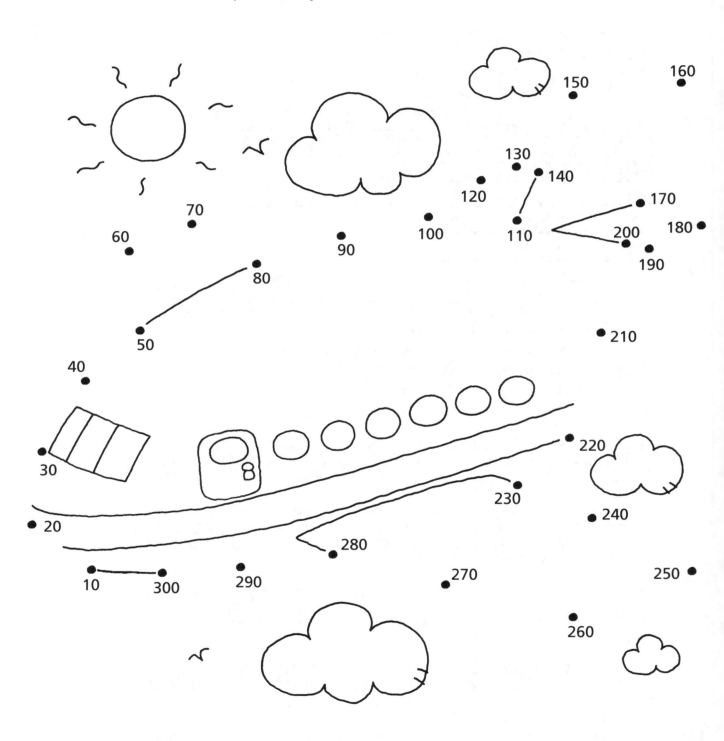

Big Blocks

Write how many hundreds, tens, and ones.

	Hundreds	Tens	Ones
1.	___	___	___
2.	___	___	___
3.	___	___	___
4.	___	___	___
5.	___	___	___
6.	___	___	___
7.	___	___	___
8.	___	___	___
9.	___	___	___
10.	___	___	___

Trains on Track

Write the missing numbers to complete the number lines.

1. | 34 | 35 | | 37 | 38 | | 40 |

2. | 58 | | 60 | | 62 | | 64 |

3. | 43 | | | 46 | 47 | | 49 |

4. | | 71 | | 73 | | 75 | |

5. | | | 30 | 31 | 32 | | |

6. | 66 | | | | 70 | |

7. | | | | 14 | | | 17 |

8. | 94 | | | | | | |

9. | | 86 | | 88 | 89 | | |

10. | | | 50 | | | | |

Cabin Numbers

Write the missing numbers to complete the number lines.

1.

2.

3.

4.

5.

6.

7.

8.

9.

10.

Hopping with Hundreds

Skip count by 2s.

1. 100   102   104   106   _____   _____

2. 374   376   378   _____   _____   _____

3. 423   425   427   _____   _____   _____

4. 661   663   _____   _____   _____   _____

5. 898   900   _____   _____   _____   _____

6. 517   519   _____   _____   _____   _____

7. 284   _____   _____   _____   _____   _____

8. 989   _____   _____   _____   _____   _____

9. 760   _____   _____   _____   _____   _____

10. 495   _____   _____   _____   _____   _____

Biking to the Beach

It's easy to get lost in this town! Help Ryan find the beach. Skip count by 5s.

Greater Grapes

Count the grapes in each bunch. Write the number on the line.
Circle the bunch with the greater number of grapes.

1.

_____   _____

2.

_____   _____

3.

_____   _____

4.

_____   _____

5.

_____   _____

6.

_____   _____

7.

_____   _____

8.

_____   _____

9.

_____   _____

10.

_____   _____

Blocks and a Box

Count the hundreds, tens, and ones. Compare the groups. Write **<**, **>**, or **=** in each box.

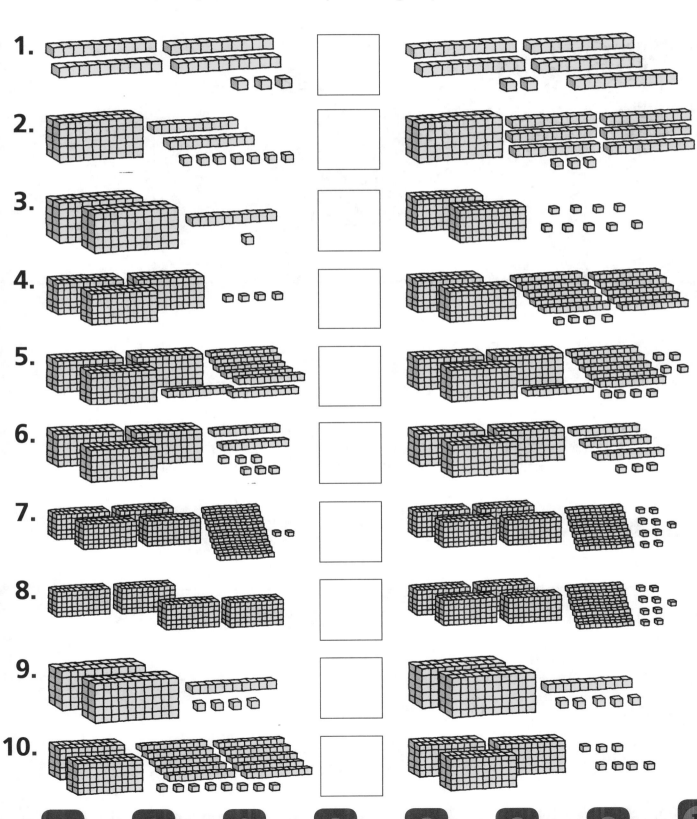

1.

2.

3.

4.

5.

6.

7.

8.

9.

10.

Hungry Hippo

Compare the numbers. Write **<**, **>**, or **=** in each box.

1. 27 ☐ 24

2. 55 ☐ 58

3. 34 ☐ 44

4. 76 ☐ 61

5. 89 ☐ 97

6. 15 ☐ 3

7. 42 ☐ 42

8. 59 ☐ 38

9. 20 ☐ 16

10. 74 ☐ 55

Picky Pelican

Compare the numbers. Write **<**, **>**, or **=** in each box.

1. 263 ☐ 266

2. 314 ☐ 309

3. 625 ☐ 526

4. 480 ☐ 508

5. 123 ☐ 97

6. 762 ☐ 772

7. 949 ☐ 950

8. 638 ☐ 638

9. 851 ☐ 842

10. 170 ☐ 207

Compare and Color

Color the areas that are true.

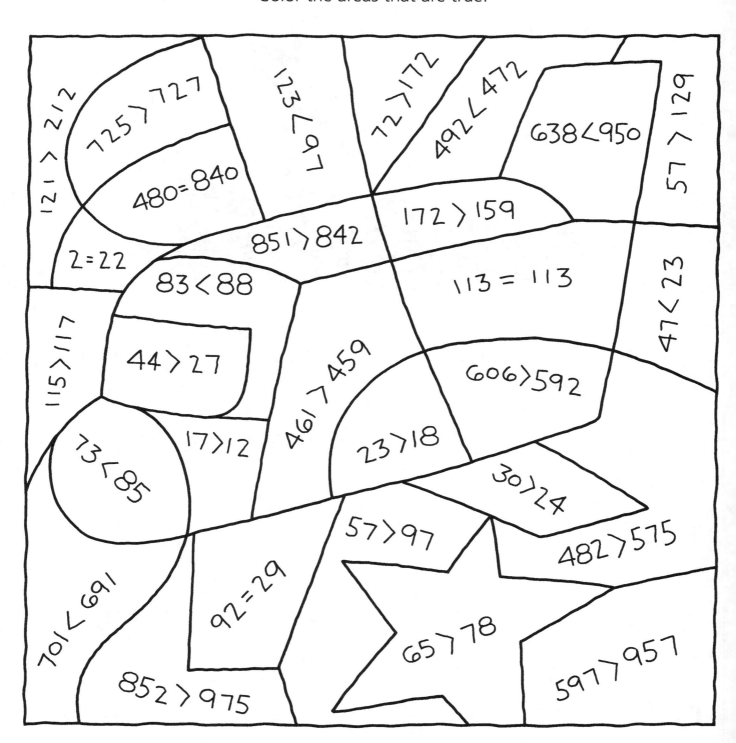

Sandy Surprise

Solve the problems. Then write your answers on the lines.

1. Jessica fills a pail with sand. She finds 23 tiny shells in it. How many groups of 10 can the shells make? _____ How many 1s are left? _____

2. Jessica and her brother, James, look for more shells. They make 4 piles that each have 100 shells. They also have 1 pile of 10 shells and 1 pile of 8 shells. How many shells did Jessica and James find in all?

_____

3. James and Jessica sort the shells into white shells and colorful shells. The white pile has 307 shells. The colorful pile has 111 shells. Which pile has more shells? Compare the numbers and use the symbols **<**, **>**, or **=**.

_____

Show and Shell

Find even more shells! Count and add the shells. Write the sum on the line.

1. + = _____

2.  +  = _____

3. + = _____

4.  +  = _____

5.  +  = _____

6. 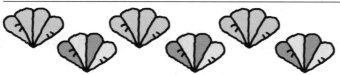 +  = _____

7.  +  = _____

8.  + = _____

9.  +  = _____

10.  +    = _____

Sum in the Sun

Add the numbers. Write the sum in the sun.

1. 6
+ 3

2. 9
+ 1

3. 4
+ 8

4. 7
+ 7

5. 2
+ 5

6. 1
+ 8

7. 3
+ 9

8. 5
+ 6

9. 0
+ 7

10. 8
+ 7

Don't Get Wet!

Add the numbers. Use the sums to solve the riddle.

1. $\begin{array}{r} 12 \\ +\ 5 \\ \hline \end{array}$ = O

2. $\begin{array}{r} 60 \\ +\ 3 \\ \hline \end{array}$ = G

3. $\begin{array}{r} 54 \\ +\ 4 \\ \hline \end{array}$ = R

4. $\begin{array}{r} 29 \\ +\ 0 \\ \hline \end{array}$ = E

5. $\begin{array}{r} 81 \\ +\ 7 \\ \hline \end{array}$ = P

6. $\begin{array}{r} 42 \\ +\ 2 \\ \hline \end{array}$ = L

7. $\begin{array}{r} 91 \\ +\ 1 \\ \hline \end{array}$ = S

8. $\begin{array}{r} 13 \\ +\ 3 \\ \hline \end{array}$ = A

9. $\begin{array}{r} 75 \\ +\ 4 \\ \hline \end{array}$ = N

10. $\begin{array}{r} 30 \\ +\ 0 \\ \hline \end{array}$ = W

What is full of holes but can hold lots of water?

___   ___ ___   ___ ___   ___ ___
16   92   88   17   79   63   29

Rainy Regrouping

Add the numbers. Write the answers in the raindrops.

Here is how to regroup:

$$\begin{array}{r} {\scriptstyle 1} \\ 28 \\ + \ 8 \\ \hline 36 \end{array}$$

Add the ones. $8 + 8 = 16$.

Give the 1 ten to the tens and add. $1 + 2 = 3$.

1. $\begin{array}{r} 13 \\ + \ 9 \\ \hline \end{array}$

2. $\begin{array}{r} 56 \\ + \ 4 \\ \hline \end{array}$

3. $\begin{array}{r} 38 \\ + \ 8 \\ \hline \end{array}$

4. $\begin{array}{r} 25 \\ + \ 6 \\ \hline \end{array}$

5. $\begin{array}{r} 77 \\ + \ 7 \\ \hline \end{array}$

6. $\begin{array}{r} 49 \\ + \ 1 \\ \hline \end{array}$

7. $\begin{array}{r} 86 \\ + \ 7 \\ \hline \end{array}$

8. $\begin{array}{r} 63 \\ + \ 9 \\ \hline \end{array}$

9. $\begin{array}{r} 27 \\ + \ 8 \\ \hline \end{array}$

10. $\begin{array}{r} 94 \\ + \ 9 \\ \hline \end{array}$

Swings for Sophia

Help Sophia find the swings in the park.
Follow the addition problems that need regrouping.

Charlie and the Chickens

Use addition to solve the problems. You may need to regroup. Show your work.

1. Charlie has 45 chickens. He will buy 4 more chickens. How many chickens will he have in all?

2. Charlie counted the new eggs. There are 33 white eggs and 8 brown eggs. How many new eggs are there altogether?

3. Charlie sees 9 eggs with chicks about to come out. There are already 27 chicks. How many chicks will he have after the new chicks come out?

Flashy Farm

Use the bar graph to answer the questions. Show your work.

ANIMALS AT FLASHY FARM

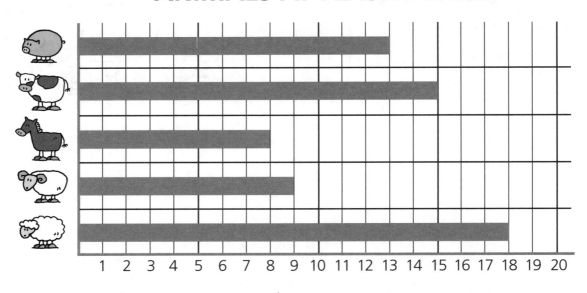

1. How many horses are at Flashy Farm? _____

2. The goats and sheep sleep in one big pen. How many animals sleep together in the pen? _____

3. Eight piglets were just born! Now how many pigs are there? _____

Empty Eggs

Count the eggs in the nest. Subtract the eggs with chicks coming out.
Write the difference on the line.

1.

 − 🐤🐤 = _____

2.

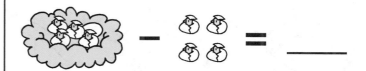 − 🐤🐤🐤🐤 = _____

3.

 − 🐤 = _____

4.

− 🐤🐤 = _____

5.

 − 🐤🐤🐤🐤🐤 = _____

6.

− 🐤🐤 = _____

7.

 − 🐤🐤🐤 = _____

8.

 − 🐤🐤 = _____

9.

 − 🐤🐤🐤🐤 = _____

10.

− 🐤🐤🐤🐤🐤🐤 = _____

Wheel Away

Subtract the numbers. Write the differences inside each wheelbarrow.

1.   3
     − 2

2.   5
     − 3

3.   2
     − 1

4.   6
     − 2

5.   8
     − 5

6.   7
     − 2

7.   4
     − 0

8.   9
     − 3

9.   9
     − 7

10.   8
     − 1

Find a Friend

Color the areas with differences of 13.

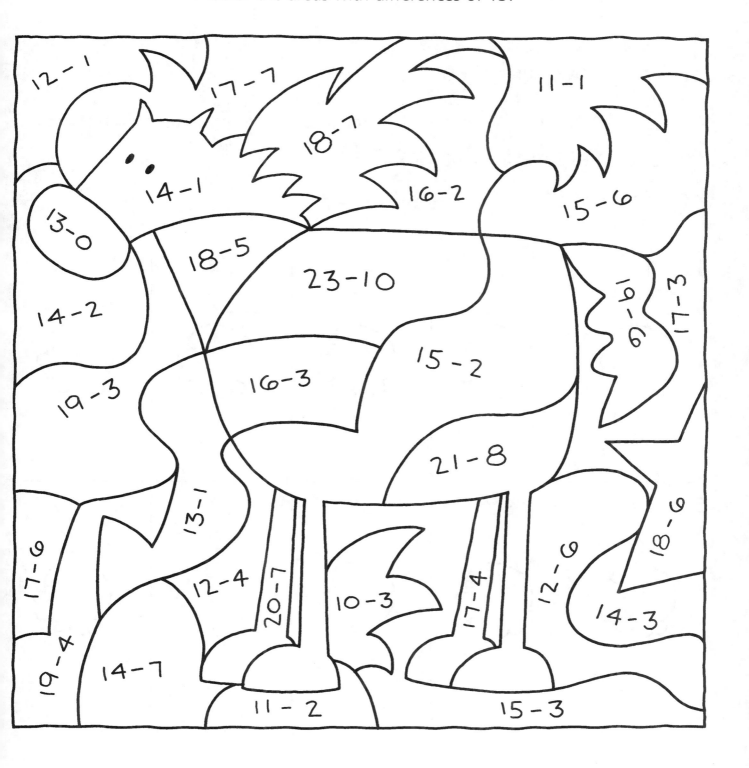

Subtraction Snack

Subtract the numbers. Write the difference in the popcorn.

Here is how to regroup:

$$\begin{array}{r} {}^{2}\!\!\not{3}{}^{1}\!4 \\ -\ \ 9 \\ \hline 25 \end{array}$$

To subtract the ones, you must take 1 from the tens. $14 - 9 = 5$.

Now subtract the tens. $2 - 0 = 2$.

1. $\begin{array}{r} 13 \\ -\ 8 \\ \hline \end{array}$

2. $\begin{array}{r} 25 \\ -\ 7 \\ \hline \end{array}$

3. $\begin{array}{r} 41 \\ -\ 2 \\ \hline \end{array}$

4. $\begin{array}{r} 64 \\ -\ 7 \\ \hline \end{array}$

5. $\begin{array}{r} 30 \\ -\ 4 \\ \hline \end{array}$

6. $\begin{array}{r} 72 \\ -\ 8 \\ \hline \end{array}$

7. $\begin{array}{r} 98 \\ -\ 9 \\ \hline \end{array}$

8. $\begin{array}{r} 56 \\ -\ 8 \\ \hline \end{array}$

9. $\begin{array}{r} 81 \\ -\ 9 \\ \hline \end{array}$

10. $\begin{array}{r} 15 \\ -\ 6 \\ \hline \end{array}$

Movie Match

Draw a line between the problems that have the same differences.

MOVIE
24
- 8

MOVIE
32
- 7

MOVIE
11
- 3

MOVIE
43
- 7

MOVIE
25
- 6

14
- 6
TICKET

22
- 6
TICKET

28
- 9
TICKET

34
- 9
TICKET

40
- 4
TICKET

Monday Movie

Use subtraction to solve the problems. You may need to regroup. Show your work.

1. The movie begins in 15 minutes. It takes Haley and Ashley 5 minutes to walk there. How many minutes are left?

2. Each ticket costs $8. Ashley has $24. How much money will she have left?

3. Haley buys a box of 30 gummy bears. She eats 7 of them before the movie begins. How many gummy bears are left?

Candy Code

Use the code to solve the subtraction problems. Remember to regroup. Show your work.

C = 14   N = 8   Y = 53   O = 22
A = 76   D = 9   B = 7   X = 6

1. C – D =

2. O – N =

3. Y – N =

4. A – B =

5. Y – D =

6. O – X =

7. C – B =

8. A – D =

9. Y – B =

10. C – X =

Jelly Bean Jars

Everyone in your class gets two jars of jelly beans.
Add the numbers to tell how many jelly beans each student receives.

1.   15
  + 21

2.   33
  + 16

3.   28
  + 40

4.   36
  + 52

5.   70
  + 20

6.   66
  + 11

7.   22
  + 31

8.   95
  + 14

9.   46
  + 43

10.   51
  + 15

Yum-Yum Sums

Add the numbers. Remember to regroup. Write the sums in the cones.

1.
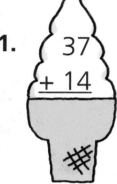
$$\begin{array}{r} 37 \\ + 14 \\ \hline \end{array}$$

2.

$$\begin{array}{r} 26 \\ + 48 \\ \hline \end{array}$$

3.

$$\begin{array}{r} 59 \\ + 36 \\ \hline \end{array}$$

4.

$$\begin{array}{r} 75 \\ + 18 \\ \hline \end{array}$$

5.

$$\begin{array}{r} 24 \\ + 16 \\ \hline \end{array}$$

6.

$$\begin{array}{r} 32 \\ + 49 \\ \hline \end{array}$$

7.

$$\begin{array}{r} 63 \\ + 27 \\ \hline \end{array}$$

8.

$$\begin{array}{r} 14 \\ + 58 \\ \hline \end{array}$$

9.
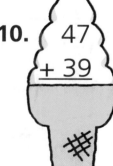
$$\begin{array}{r} 39 \\ + 28 \\ \hline \end{array}$$

10.
$$\begin{array}{r} 47 \\ + 39 \\ \hline \end{array}$$

Quick Trick

If the sum is 77, color the area brown. If the sum is 88, color the area red.
If the sum is 99, color the area gray.

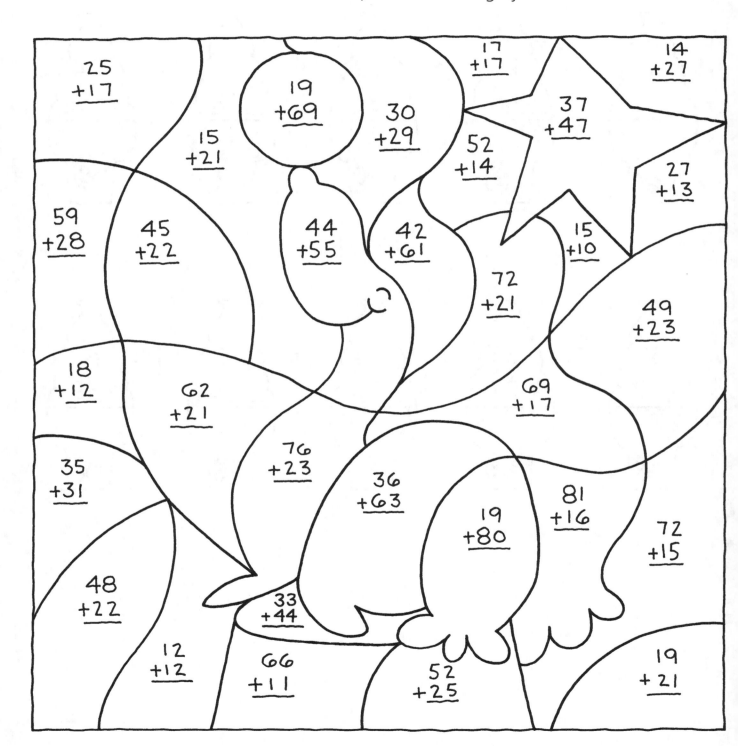

Picking Up Peanuts

Ella the elephant is fed a lot of peanuts. Later she finds more on the ground.
Add the numbers to tell how many peanuts Ella eats in all.

1. 172
+ 13

2. 405
+ 90

3. 266
+ 12

4. 534
+ 20

5. 621
+ 41

6. 304
+ 35

7. 710
+ 10

8. 925
+ 21

9. 203
+ 14

10. 868
+ 31

Juggling Act Addition

Add the numbers. You may need to regroup twice. Write the answer in the ball.

1. 317
 + 44

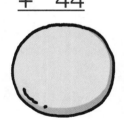

2. 816
 + 59

3. 205
 + 87

4. 943
 + 19

5. 728
 + 28

6. 664
 + 79

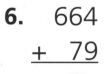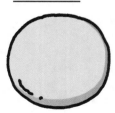

7. 458
 + 43

8. 126
 + 94

9. 575
 + 45

10. 228
 + 88

Regrouping Race

Find your seat before the circus begins! Follow the problems with sums of 789.
Work as fast as you can.

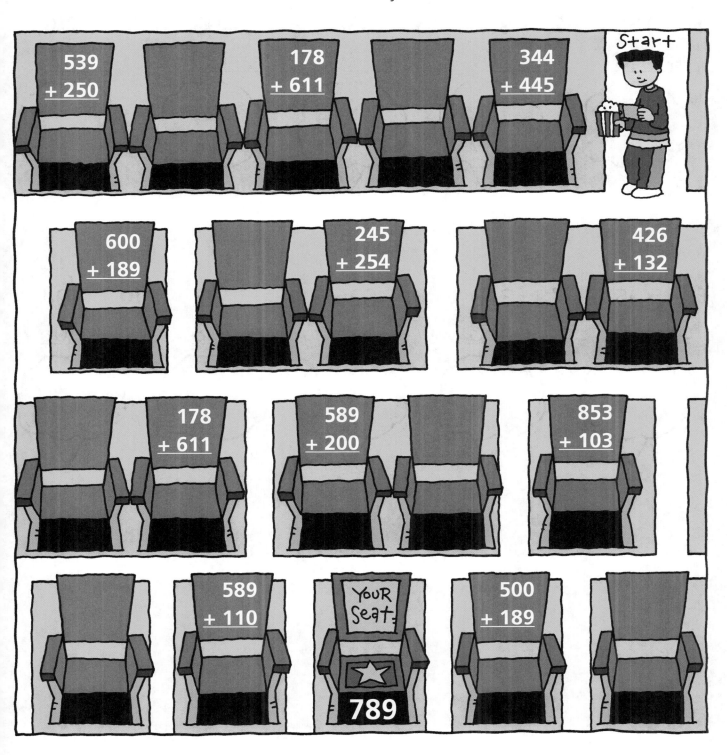

539
+ 250

178
+ 611

344
+ 445

Start

600
+ 189

245
+ 254

426
+ 132

178
+ 611

589
+ 200

853
+ 103

589
+ 110

YOUR Seat

789

500
+ 189

Sweet Sums

Add the numbers. Watch out for regrouping. Write the answer in the cotton candy.

1. 158
+ 114

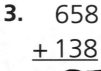

2. 306
+ 207

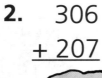

3. 658
+ 138

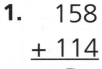

4. 499
+ 499

5. 278
+ 557

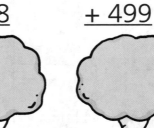

6. 705
+ 199

7. 349
+ 468

8. 626
+ 576

9. 737
+ 778

10. 494
+ 906

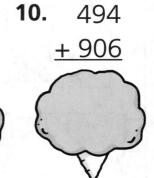

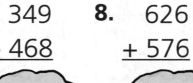

Roaring Riddle

Add the numbers. You may need to regroup. Use the sums to answer the riddle.

1. 28 + 36 = N	**2.** 195 + 70 = E	**3.** 288 + 19 = M	**4.** 34 + 87 = P	**5.** 506 + 429 = S
6. 936 + 75 = A	**7.** 612 + 200 = R	**8.** 84 + 58 = L	**9.** 752 + 490 = T	**10.** 268 + 31 = E

Where do lions go after the circus show?

___ ___ ___ ___   ___ ___ ___ ___ ___ ___
307 1,011 64 299   935 1,242 812 265 299 1,242

Fun Field Trip

Use addition to solve the problems. You may need to regroup. Show your work.

1. The whole second grade is going to the circus! There are 27 students in one class and 28 students in the other class. How many second graders are going in total?

2. The students arrive at the big top before anyone else. They sit in their seats. There are 195 seats still empty. How many seats does the big top have in all?
   (Hint: Use your answer from #1.)

3. The circus sold 242 tickets on that day. It sold only 179 the next day. How many tickets did the circus sell over those 2 days?

Pigeons in the Park

Subtract the numbers to tell how many pigeons fly away from each group.

1. 22
     − 11

2. 35
     − 33

3. 50
     − 20

4. 78
     − 50

5. 46
     − 12

6. 89
     − 44

7. 63
     − 10

8. 27
     − 26

9. 88
     −12

10. 91
      − 10

Seesaw Subtraction

Draw a line between the problems that have the same difference.
Remember to regroup.

93
− 39

65
− 48

24
− 16

42
− 23

91
− 59

86
− 78

81
− 27

60
− 28

36
− 19

75
− 56

Mirror, Mirror

Subtract the numbers. Remember to regroup.

1. 84
     − 48

2. 53
     − 35

3. 73
     − 37

4. 41
     − 14

5. 95
     − 59

6. 32
     − 23

7. 61
     − 16

8. 82
     − 28

9. 96
     − 69

10. 71
      − 17

Good Catch!

Subtract the numbers. Write the difference in the baseball glove.

1.   157
   − 23

2.   482
   − 60

3.   729
   − 14

4.   310
   − 10

5.   649
   − 33

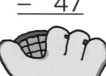

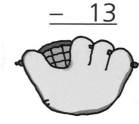

6.   588
   − 47

7.   265
   − 11

8.   847
   − 20

9.   182
   − 71

10.   766
   − 13

Subtract and Slide

Subtract the numbers. You may need to regroup more than once.

1. 556
   - 37

2. 294
   - 48

3. 670
   - 52

4. 183
   - 26

5. 351
   - 67

6. 822
   - 39

7. 410
   - 45

8. 996
   - 78

9. 642
   - 83

10. 470
    - 19

Hide and Honk

If you can subtract without regrouping, color the area green. If you need to regroup once, color the area blue. If you need to regroup twice, color the area yellow.

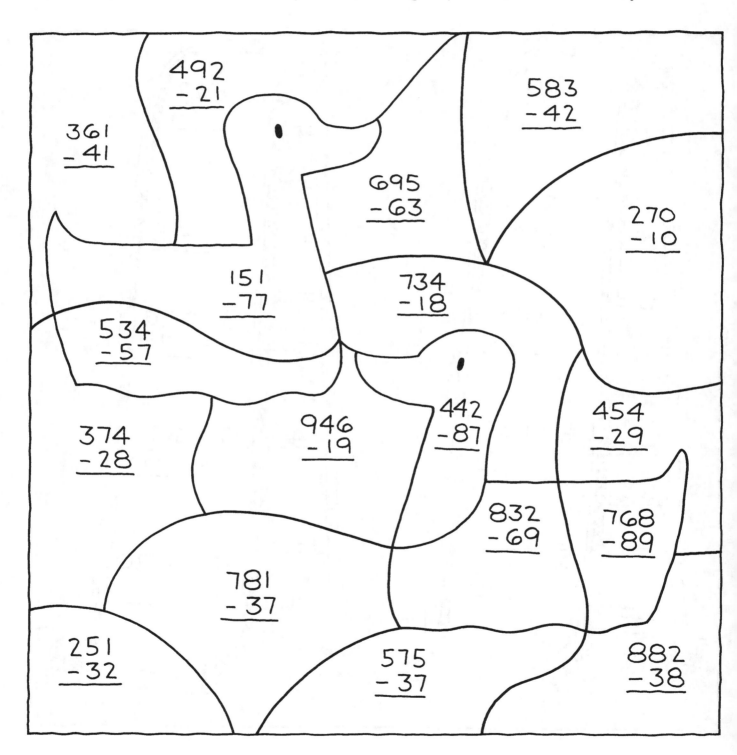

Three-Pointers

Subtract the numbers. Write the differences in the basketballs.

1. 474
− 132

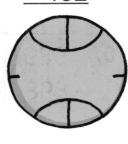

2. 816
− 611

3. 790
− 350

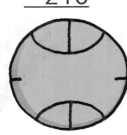

4. 522
− 210

5. 658
− 135

6. 596
− 462

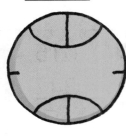

7. 959
− 801

8. 273
− 221

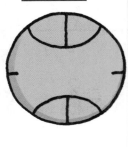

9. 601
− 300

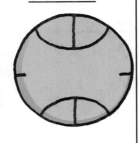

10. 873
− 333

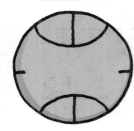

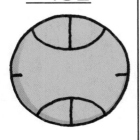

Dirty Differences

Danny got his toys very dirty. Help him clean these numbers and subtract.
You may need to regroup more than once!

1.   241
    − 127

2.   580
    − 354

3.   768
    − 329

4.   941
    − 678

5.   492
    − 487

6.   706
    − 259

7.   831
    − 526

8.   370
    − 237

9.   615
    − 347

10.   989
     − 898

What Was the Weather?

The bar graph shows the weather from last year. Use the graph and subtraction to answer the questions. You may need to regroup. Show your work.

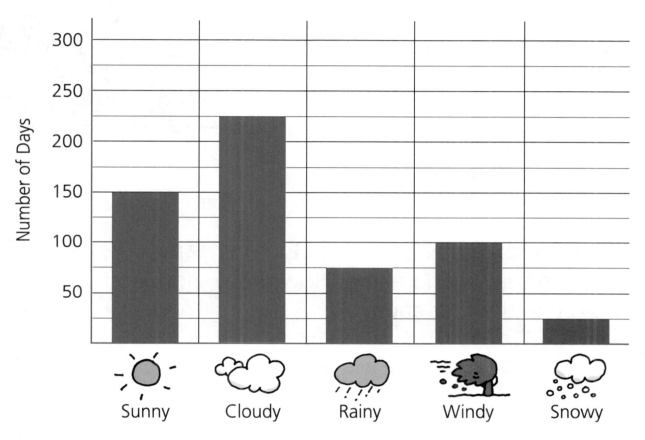

WEATHER REPORT

1. How many more cloudy days were there than sunny days?

2. How many cloudy days were not rainy?

3. There are 365 days in a year. How many days last year weren't snowy?

Pin Problems

Use subtraction to solve the problems. You may need to regroup more than once. Show your work.

1. The Garcia family went bowling last night. Carlos scored 87 points. Mrs. Garcia bowled 153 points. How many more points did Mrs. Garcia score?

2. The Garcias scored 591 points in the first game. They scored only 423 in the second game. How many more points did they score in the first game?

3. The top score at the bowling alley is 280. Maria's best score is 194. How many points does she need to reach the top score?

Think Fast!

Add or subtract the numbers. See how fast you can finish the page.
Watch out for regrouping!

1. 83
     + 9

2. 40
     − 10

3. 82
     − 37

4. 51
     + 66

5. 28
     − 0

6. 93
     − 74

7. 35
     + 5

8. 16
     − 9

9. 84
     − 58

10. 11
      + 99

Museum Maze

Samantha is lost in the museum! Her family is waiting at the dinosaurs. Follow the problems with sums or differences of 58.

Ping-Pong

Write each addition problem as two subtraction problems.

1. 3
   + 7
   10

2. 14
   + 8
   22

3. 35
   + 11
   46

4. 82
   + 5
   87

5. 40
   + 61
   101

Playing Pool

Write each subtraction problem as two addition problems.

1.
$$\begin{array}{r} 6 \\ -\ 4 \\ \hline 2 \end{array}$$

2.
$$\begin{array}{r} 17 \\ -\ 8 \\ \hline 9 \end{array}$$

3.
$$\begin{array}{r} 255 \\ -\ 40 \\ \hline 215 \end{array}$$

 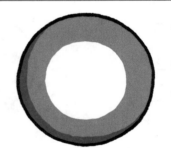

4.
$$\begin{array}{r} 61 \\ -\ 58 \\ \hline 3 \end{array}$$

5.
$$\begin{array}{r} 102 \\ -\ 27 \\ \hline 75 \end{array}$$

Pick a Pair

Jasmine needs to find pairs of cards.
Draw a line between cards with the same sum or difference.

6 + 9	99 − 72
42 − 15	95 + 96
83 + 58	10 + 46
602 − 546	9 + 6
271 − 80	111 + 30

At the Arcade

Use addition or subtraction to solve the problems. Watch out for regrouping! Show your work.

1. Joseph and Dylan take turns playing pinball. Joseph scores 263 points. Dylan hits the big bonus and scores 718 points. How many points do they score in total?

2. Isabella's favorite game is skeeball. She scores 440 points this time! Her top score is 520. How many points away is her top score?

3. After an hour, Joseph has 2 prize tickets, Dylan has 5 prize tickets, and Isabella has 3 prize tickets. A big, bouncy ball costs 9 prize tickets. Do they have enough tickets altogether to buy the bouncy ball?

Multiplying with Michael

Write each multiplication problem as a long addition problem. Find the sum.

Michael knows that 2 × 3 is the same as adding 2 three times, like this: 2 + 2 + 2. That sum is 6, and so 2 × 3 is 6, too.

1. 4 × 2

2. 3 × 4

3. 5 × 3

4. 2 × 4

5. 1 × 5

6. 6 × 3

7. 4 × 5

8. 5 × 4

9. 2 × 6

10. 3 × 7

More Multiplying

Color the blocks to show the multiplication. Write the answer on the line.
The first one is done for you.

1.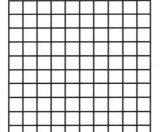

$4 \times 2 =$

_8_

2.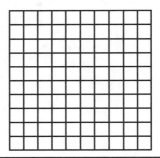

$3 \times 5 =$

_____

3.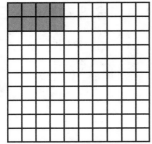

$7 \times 4 =$

_____

4.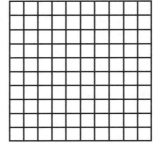

$2 \times 8 =$

_____

5.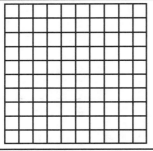

$5 \times 2 =$

_____

6.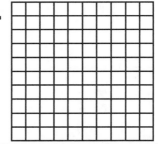

$6 \times 3 =$

_____

7.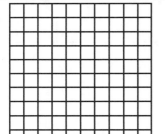

$4 \times 5 =$

_____

8.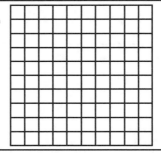

$7 \times 6 =$

_____

9.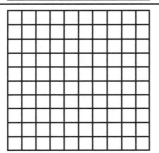

$8 \times 7 =$

_____

10.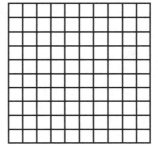

$4 \times 9 =$

_____

Dividing with Danielle

Write each division problem as a long subtraction problem.
Then write the answer to the division problem.

Danielle baked 12 cookies. She wants to give the same number of cookies to her 3 friends. She knows that 12 cookies divided for 3 people is the same as counting how many times 3 can be subtracted from 12, like $12 - 3 - 3 - 3 - 3 = 0$. Since 3 can be subtracted 4 times, then $12 \div 3 = 4$.

1. $4 \div 2$

2. $10 \div 5$

3. $12 \div 4$

4. $6 \div 3$

5. $8 \div 4$

6. $15 \div 5$

7. $20 \div 5$

8. $14 \div 2$

9. $16 \div 4$

10. $20 \div 10$

Bunches of Balloons

Draw and color balloons to show the division. Write the answer on the line. The first one is done for you.

1. 10 ÷ 2 = __5__

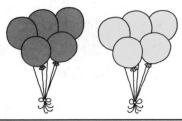

2. 12 ÷ 2 = _____

3. 8 ÷ 4 = _____

4. 15 ÷ 5 = _____

5. 20 ÷ 4 = _____

6. 30 ÷ 6 = _____

7. 18 ÷ 3 = _____

8. 9 ÷ 3 = _____

9. 16 ÷ 4 = _____

10. 10 ÷ 5 = _____

To the Zoo

Use addition or multiplication to solve the problems. Show your work.

1. The class makes groups of 6 students each. There are 4 groups in all. How many students are in the class?

2. The students love to watch the monkeys. There are 5 trees with monkeys playing. There are 3 monkeys in each tree. How many monkeys are there in all?

3. Sharks are scary! There are only 2 sharks in each big tank. There are 4 tanks. How many sharks are at the zoo?

Pizza Party

Use subtraction or division to solve the problems. Show your work.

1. Kayla is having 30 kids at her birthday party. There are 5 boxes of pizza. How many kids need to share each box of pizza?

2. Everyone should have the same number of pizza slices. Each pizza box has 12 slices. How many slices can each kid eat? (Hint: Use the answer from #1.)

3. There are 60 slices of pizza in total. There are 10 tables. How many slices of pizza should go to each table?

Maze of Mess

Chris needs to do his homework before dinner. Help him find his math book.
Follow the multiplication problems with answers that get greater by 5.

Fruity Fractions

Color the orange to show the fraction. The first one is done for you.

1. $\dfrac{1}{2}$

2. $\dfrac{1}{4}$
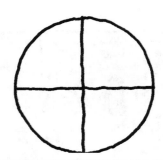

3. $\dfrac{1}{3}$
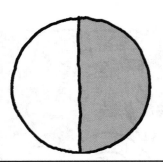

4. $\dfrac{2}{3}$

5. $\dfrac{3}{4}$
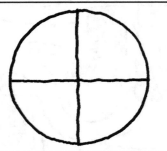

6. $\dfrac{2}{5}$

7. $\dfrac{4}{8}$
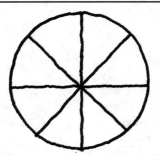

8. $\dfrac{3}{6}$
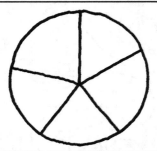

9. $\dfrac{5}{6}$
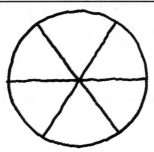

10. $\dfrac{1}{10}$
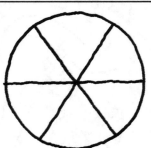

Figure the Fraction

Write the fraction shown.

1.  _____

2.  _____

3. 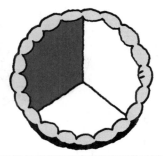 _____

4.  _____

5. 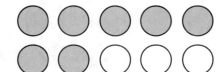 _____

6.  _____

7. 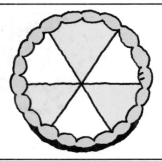 _____

8.  _____

9. 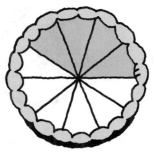 _____

10.  _____

Eye the Pies

Write the fraction under each pie. Then write **<**, **>**, or **=** in the box.

1.

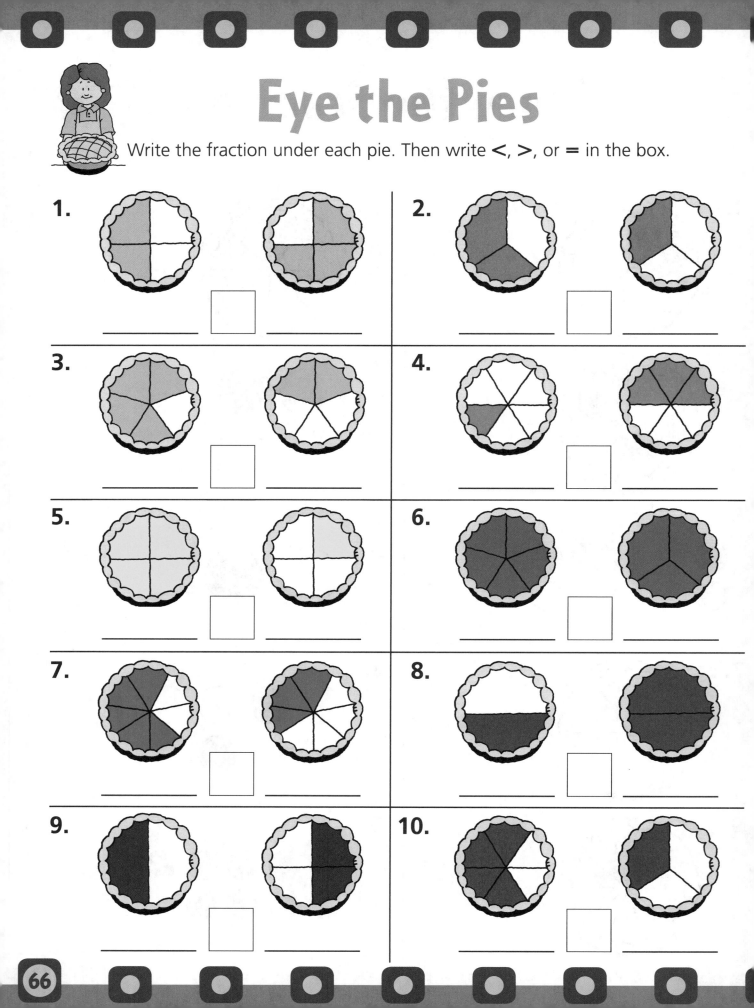

_____   ☐   _____

2.

_____   ☐   _____

3.

_____   ☐   _____

4.

_____   ☐   _____

5.

_____   ☐   _____

6.

_____   ☐   _____

7.

_____   ☐   _____

8.

_____   ☐   _____

9.

_____   ☐   _____

10.

_____   ☐   _____

Huge and Whole

Find the fractions that are the same as one whole. Color those areas gray.

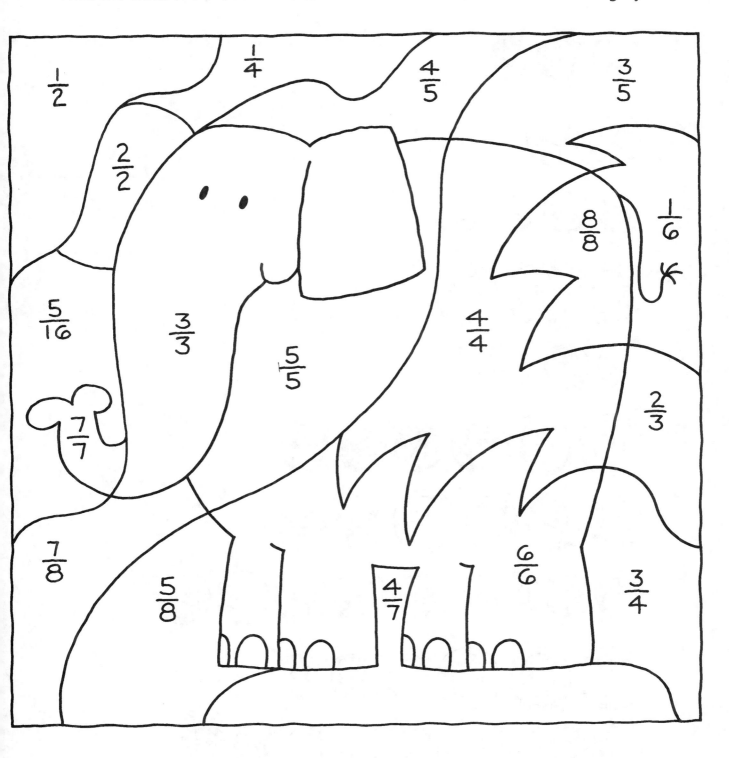

$\frac{1}{2}$ $\frac{1}{4}$ $\frac{4}{5}$ $\frac{3}{5}$

$\frac{2}{2}$

$\frac{8}{8}$ $\frac{1}{6}$

$\frac{5}{16}$ $\frac{3}{3}$ $\frac{5}{5}$ $\frac{4}{4}$

$\frac{2}{3}$

$\frac{7}{7}$

$\frac{7}{8}$ $\frac{5}{8}$ $\frac{4}{7}$ $\frac{6}{6}$ $\frac{3}{4}$

Counting Coins

Count the coins. Write the total amount of money on the line.

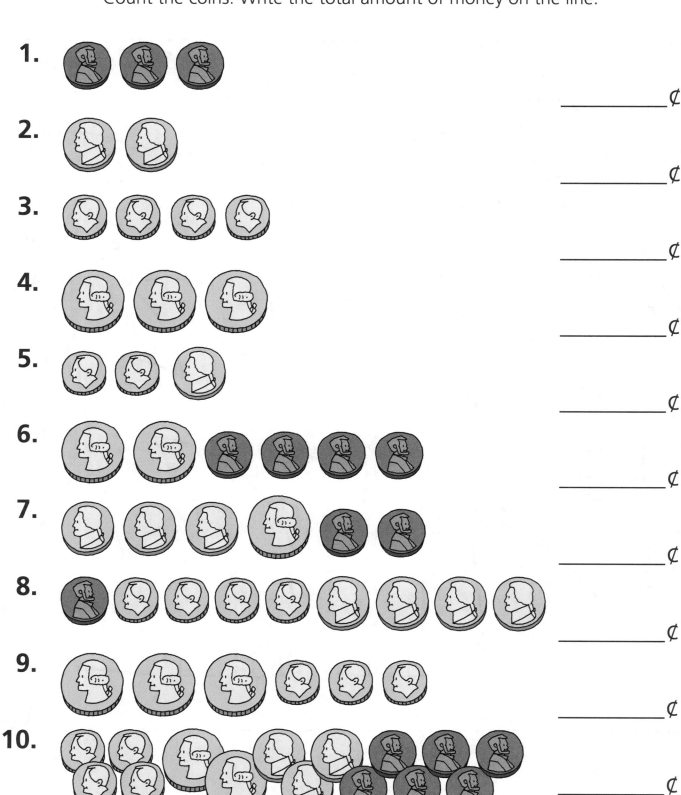

1. _____ ¢

2. _____ ¢

3. _____ ¢

4. _____ ¢

5. _____ ¢

6. _____ ¢

7. _____ ¢

8. _____ ¢

9. _____ ¢

10. _____ ¢

Dollars and Cents

Count the bills and coins. Write the total amount of money on the line.

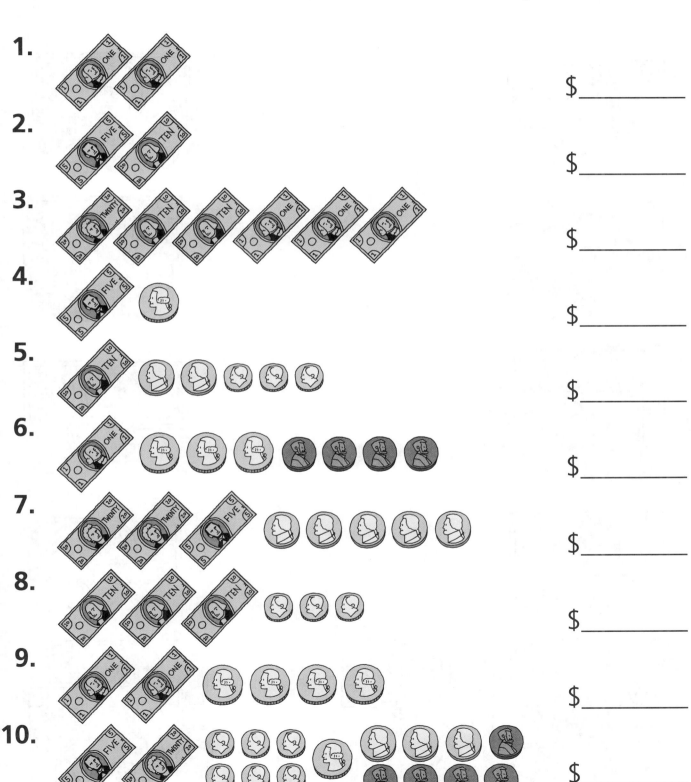

1. $_____

2. $_____

3. $_____

4. $_____

5. $_____

6. $_____

7. $_____

8. $_____

9. $_____

10. $_____

Matching Money

Draw a line between the groups that have the same amount of money.

Summer Sale

Circle the bills and coins you need to buy each item.

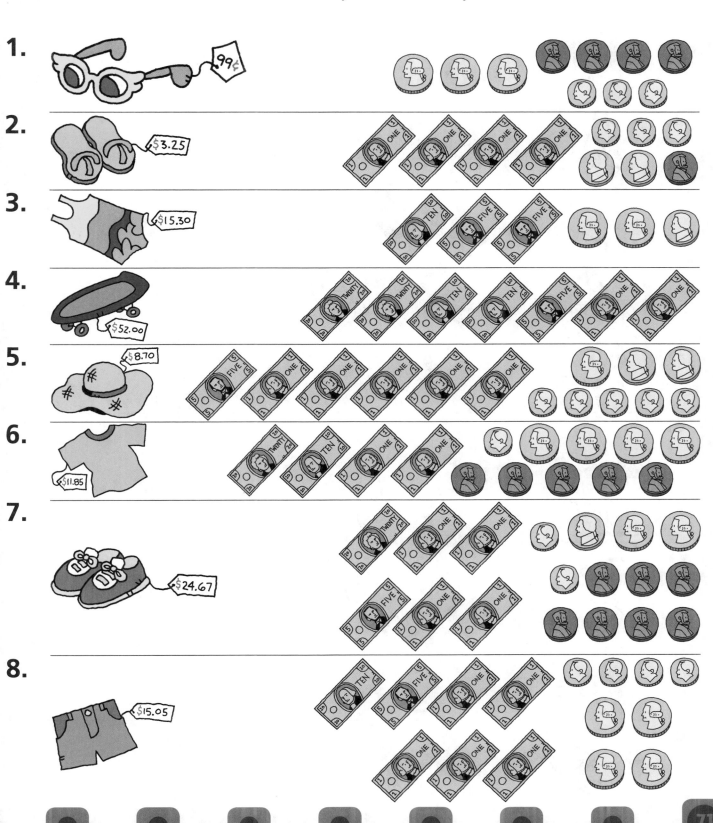

1. .99¢

2. $3.25

3. $15.30

4. $52.00

5. $8.70

6. $11.85

7. $24.67

8. $15.05

Garden Gear

Draw the fewest coins and bills you need to buy each item. The first one is done for you.

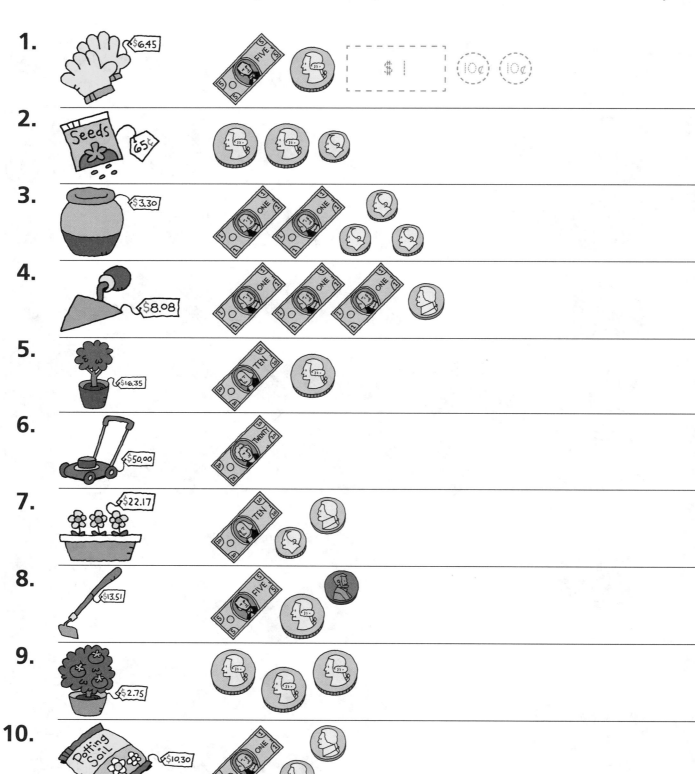

1. $6.45

2. 65¢

3. $3.30

4. $8.08

5. $16.35

6. $50.00

7. $22.17

8. $13.51

9. $2.75

10. $10.30

Sarah's Savings

Sarah is taking her saved money to the bank. Follow the bags with amounts that get greater and greater.

Ice Cream!

Use what you know about money, addition, and subtraction.
Solve the problems. Show your work.

1. Morgan wants a chocolate-covered ice-cream bar. Each bar costs 85¢. She has 3 quarters and a nickel. Does she have enough money?

2. Each mini ice-cream sandwich costs 39¢. Samuel wants to buy 2 of them. How much money does he need?

3. Alyssa can't wait to eat a strawberry ice pop. Each one costs 75¢. She gives a $1 bill to the ice-cream truck driver. How many quarters will she get in change?

Watch Match

Draw a line between the watches that show the same time.

Whole and Half Hours

Write the time shown on each clock.

1.

_____

2.

_____

3.

_____

4.

_____

5.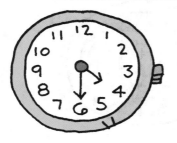

_____

6.

_____

7.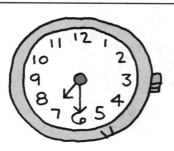

_____

8.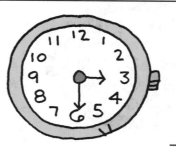

_____

9.

_____

10.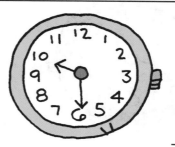

_____

Time Flies

Look at each pair of clocks. Write how many hours and minutes have passed.
The first one is done for you.

1.

I hour and 30 minutes

2.

_____ hour

3.

_____ hours and _____ minutes

4.

_____ minutes

5.

_____ hours

6.

_____ hour and _____ minutes

7.

_____ hours and _____ minutes

8.

_____ hours

9.

_____ hours

10.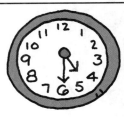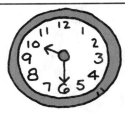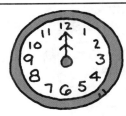

_____ hours and _____ minutes

Time Tie

Draw a line between the clocks that show the same time.

Quarter Hours

Write the time shown on each clock.

1.

_____

2.

_____

3.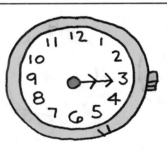

_____

4.

_____

5.

_____

6.

_____

7.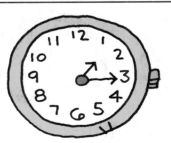

_____

8.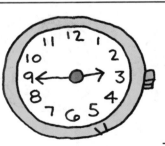

_____

9.

_____

10.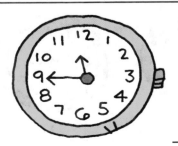

_____

Tick Tock

Look at each pair of clocks. Write how many hours and minutes have passed.
The first one is done for you.

1.

I hour and 15 minutes

2.

_____ minutes

3.

_____ minutes

4.

_____ hour and _____ minutes

5.

_____ minutes

6.

_____ hours

7.

_____ hours and _____ minutes

8.

_____ hours and _____ minutes

9.

_____ hours and _____ minutes

10.

_____ minutes

Cool in the Pool

Solve the problems.

1. Caleb is going swimming today! The town pool opens at 9:00. The clock on the wall reads 7:00. How many hours does Caleb have to wait? _____

2. Water volleyball begins at 10:30. The teams play for an hour and a half. What time does water volleyball end?

_____

3. Caleb needs to leave the pool at 3:30. His watch looks like this:

How many more minutes can he swim? _____

Clocks off the Dock

Help Howard find the treasure! Follow the clocks that show
the time getting later by 15 minutes.

Nutty Units

Use the peanuts to measure how long each food is. Each peanut is one unit.
Write the number of units on the line.

1.

about _____ units

2.

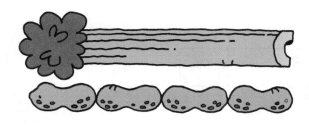

about _____ units

3.

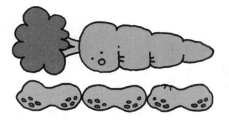

about _____ units

4.

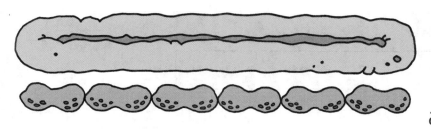

about _____ units

5.

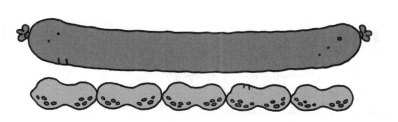

about _____ units

In Inches

Use the inch ruler to measure how long each object is.
Write the number of inches on the line.

1.

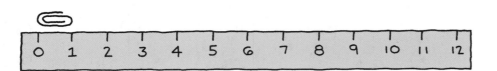

about _____ inches

2.

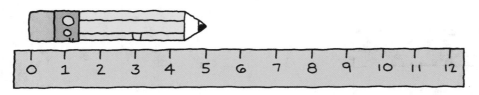

about _____ inches

3.

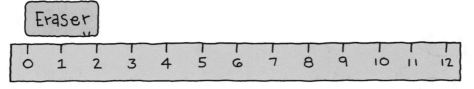

about _____ inches

4.

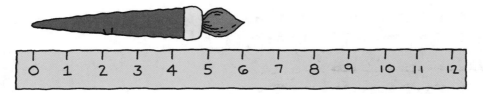

about _____ inches

5.

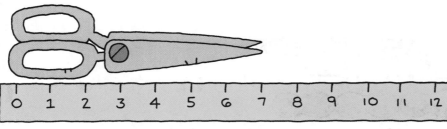

about _____ inches

Centimeter Measure

Use the centimeter ruler to measure how long each object is.
Write the number of centimeters on the line.

1.

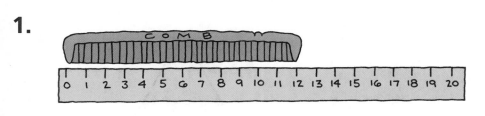

about _____ centimeters

2.

about _____ centimeters

3.

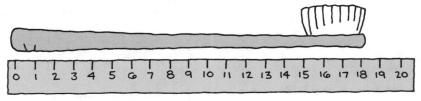

about _____ centimeters

4.

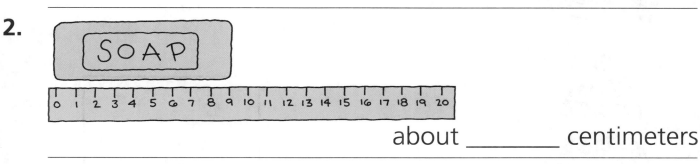

about _____ centimeters

5.

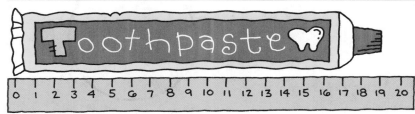

about _____ centimeters

Sort the Shapes

Draw a line between each object and its matching shape.

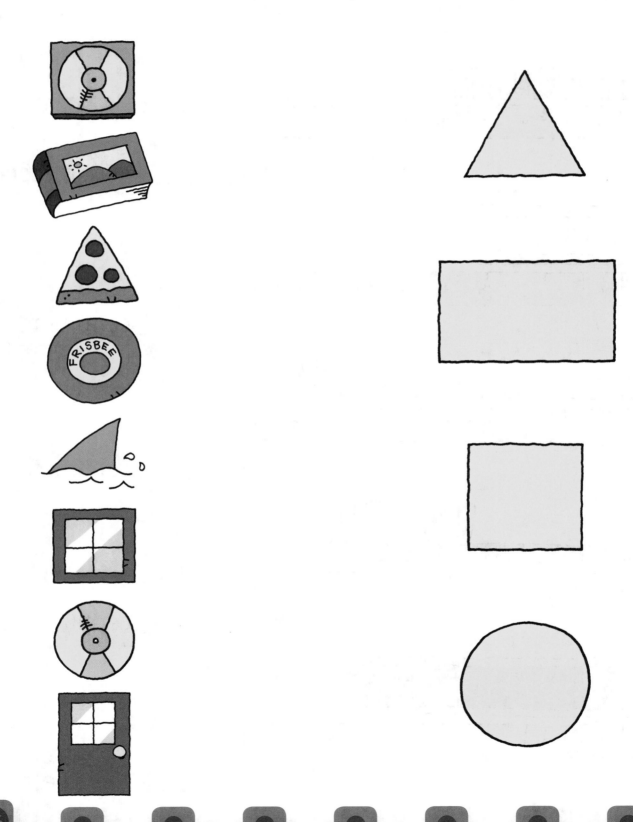

Show What You Know

Complete the shape chart. Write the name of the shape and
the number of straight sides.

Shape	Name	Sides

Solid Figures

Draw a line between each object and its matching figure.

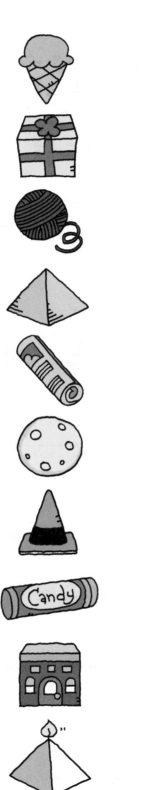

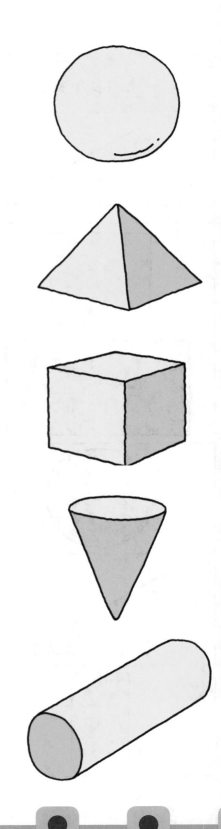

Figuring out Figures

Draw a line between each figure and its name. If the figure has flat sides, write the word **sides** on the line. If the figure has round curves, write the word **curves** on the line. If the figure has sides and curves, write the word **both** on the line.

1.

It has _____.

2.

It has _____.

3.

It has _____.

4.

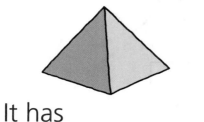

It has _____.

5.

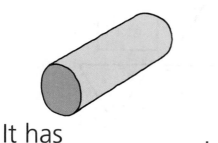

It has _____.

cone

cylinder

sphere

cube

pyramid

Shade the Shapes

Color the next shapes in the patterns.

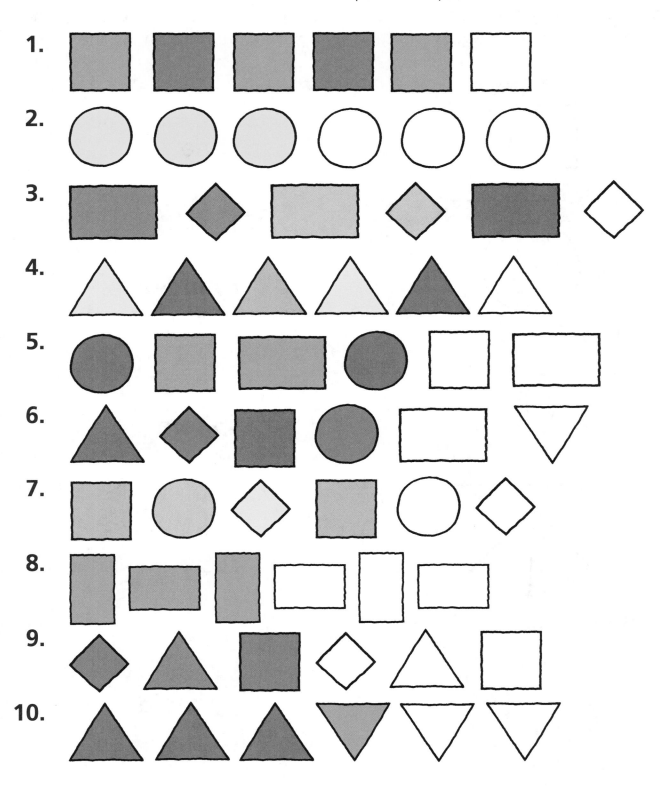

Pattern Page

Draw and color the next shapes in the patterns. Each row needs eight shapes in all.

1.

2.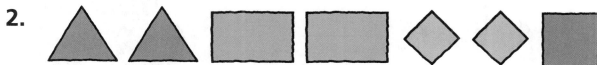

3.

4.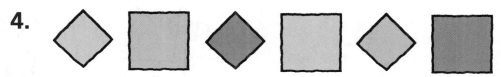

5.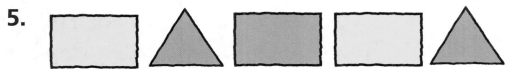

6.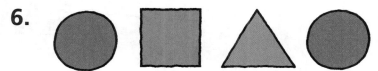

7.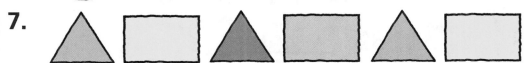

8.

9.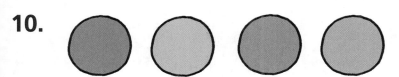

10.

Take a Number

Who's next? Write the next number in each pattern.

1. 1   2   3   4   5   _____

2. 2   4   6   8   10   12   _____

3. 3   5   7   _____

4. 1   4   7   10   13   _____

5. 5   10   15   20   _____

6. 13   23   33   _____

7. 15   19   23   27   31   35   _____

8. 40   44   48   52   56   _____

9. 2   7   12   17   22   _____

10. 85   88   91   94   97   _____

Petal Patterns

Solve the problems. You can draw a picture to help you. Write the answers on the lines.

1. Elena put pots of flowers on the windowsill. Each flower has 5 petals. How many petals in total are on the first 2 flowers? _____ How many are on the first 3 flowers? _____

2. Elena is planting rows of roses and rows of daisies. She wants to switch flowers with every new row. Elena will plant daisies in the first row and roses in the second row. What flowers will she plant in the third row? _____ What flowers will be in the sixth row? _____

3. Elena wants to plant a lot of tulips in this color pattern: yellow tulip, white tulip, pink tulip. The row can fit only 15 tulips. How many times can she plant the pattern? _____

Answer Key

Page 4

Page 5

(matching/illustration with answers)
1. 1 6
2. 3 9
3. 2 4
4. 5 0
5. 6 7
6. 9 1
7. 8 5
8. 4 2
9. 7 3
10. 5 8

Page 6

Page 7
1. 141
2. 327
3. 632
4. 594
5. 805
6. 273
7. 468
8. 750
9. 986
10. 019

Page 8
1. 36, 39
2. 59, 61, 63
3. 44, 45, 48
4. 70, 72, 74, 76
5. 28, 29, 33, 34
6. 67, 68, 69, 71, 72
7. 11, 12, 13, 15, 16
8. 95, 96, 97, 98, 99, 100
9. 85, 87, 90, 91
10. 48, 49, 51, 52, 53, 54

Page 9
1. 464, 466
2. 120, 121, 123, 124
3. 220, 223
4. 299, 301, 302
5. 889, 890, 891
6. 750, 751, 752, 754
7. 569, 572, 573
8. 99, 100, 101, 102, 103
9. 698, 699, 700, 701
10. 858, 859, 860, 861, 862

Page 10
1. 108, 110
2. 380, 382, 384
3. 429, 431, 433
4. 665, 667, 669, 671
5. 902, 904, 906, 908
6. 521, 523, 525, 527
7. 286, 288, 290, 292, 294
8. 991, 993, 995, 997, 999
9. 762, 764, 766, 768, 770
10. 497, 499, 501, 503, 505

Page 11

(maze illustration)

Page 12
1. 10, 13, circle second bunch
2. 42, 46, circle second bunch
3. 37, 33, circle first bunch
4. 27, 28, circle second bunch
5. 9, 6, circle first bunch
6. 15, 20, circle second bunch
7. 32, 34, circle second bunch
8. 21, 18, circle first bunch
9. 39, 45, circle second bunch
10. 46, 42, circle first bunch

Page 13
1. <
2. >
3. >
4. =
5. >
6. <
7. >
8. <
9. <
10. >

Page 14
1. >
2. <
3. <
4. >
5. <
6. >
7. =
8. >
9. >
10. >

Page 15
1. <
2. >
3. >
4. <
5. >
6. <
7. <
8. =
9. >
10. <

Page 16

(airplane color illustration)

Page 17
1. 2, 3
2. 418
3. 307 > 111 or 111 < 307

Page 18
1. 3
2. 5
3. 2
4. 7
5. 4
6. 8
7. 9
8. 6
9. 10
10. 7

Page 19
1. 9
2. 10
3. 12
4. 14
5. 7
6. 9
7. 12
8. 11
9. 7
10. 15

Page 20
1. 17
2. 63
3. 58
4. 29
5. 88
6. 44
7. 92
8. 16
9. 79
10. 30

Page 21
1. 22
2. 60
3. 46
4. 31
5. 84
6. 50
7. 93
8. 72
9. 35
10. 103

A SPONGE

Page 22

(maze illustration)

Page 23
1.
$$\begin{array}{r} 45 \\ +\ 4 \\ \hline 49 \end{array}$$
2.
$$\begin{array}{r} 1 \\ 33 \\ +\ 8 \\ \hline 41 \end{array}$$
3.
$$\begin{array}{r} 1 \\ 27 \\ +\ 9 \\ \hline 36 \end{array}$$

Page 24
1. 8
2.
$$\begin{array}{r} 1 \\ 18 \\ +\ 9 \\ \hline 27 \end{array}$$
3.
$$\begin{array}{r} 1 \\ 13 \\ +\ 8 \\ \hline 21 \end{array}$$

Page 25
1. 2
2. 1
3. 3
4. 5
5. 0
6. 6
7. 4
8. 8
9. 5
10. 1

Page 26
1. 1
2. 2
3. 1
4. 4
5. 3
6. 5
7. 4
8. 6
9. 2
10. 7

Page 27

Page 28
1. 5
2. 18
3. 39
4. 57
5. 26
6. 64
7. 89
8. 48
9. 72
10. 9

Page 29

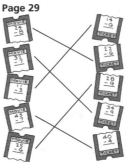

Page 30
1.
$$\begin{array}{r} 15 \\ -\ 5 \\ \hline 10 \end{array}$$
2.
$$\begin{array}{r} 1\ 1 \\ 24 \\ -\ 8 \\ \hline 16 \end{array}$$
3.
$$\begin{array}{r} 2\ 1 \\ 30 \\ -\ 7 \\ \hline 23 \end{array}$$

Page 31
1.
$$\begin{array}{r} 0\ 1 \\ 14 \\ -\ 9 \\ \hline 5 \end{array}$$
2.
$$\begin{array}{r} 1\ 1 \\ 22 \\ -\ 8 \\ \hline 14 \end{array}$$
3.
$$\begin{array}{r} 4\ 1 \\ 53 \\ -\ 8 \\ \hline 45 \end{array}$$
4.
$$\begin{array}{r} 6\ 1 \\ 76 \\ -\ 7 \\ \hline 69 \end{array}$$
5.
$$\begin{array}{r} 4\ 1 \\ 53 \\ -\ 9 \\ \hline 44 \end{array}$$
6.
$$\begin{array}{r} 1\ 1 \\ 22 \\ -\ 6 \\ \hline 16 \end{array}$$
7.
$$\begin{array}{r} 0\ 1 \\ 14 \\ -\ 7 \\ \hline 7 \end{array}$$
8.
$$\begin{array}{r} 6\ 1 \\ 76 \\ -\ 9 \\ \hline 67 \end{array}$$
9.
$$\begin{array}{r} 4\ 1 \\ 53 \\ -\ 7 \\ \hline 46 \end{array}$$
10.
$$\begin{array}{r} 0\ 1 \\ 14 \\ -\ 6 \\ \hline 8 \end{array}$$

Page 32
1. 36
2. 49
3. 68
4. 88
5. 90
6. 77
7. 53
8. 109
9. 89
10. 66

Page 33
1. 51
2. 74
3. 95
4. 93
5. 40
6. 81
7. 90
8. 72
9. 67
10. 86

Page 34

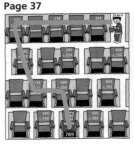

Page 35
1. 185
2. 495
3. 278
4. 554
5. 662
6. 339
7. 720
8. 946
9. 217
10. 899

Page 36
1. 361
2. 875
3. 292
4. 962
5. 756
6. 743
7. 501
8. 220
9. 620
10. 316

Page 37

(theater seats illustration)

Page 38
1. 272
2. 513
3. 796
4. 998
5. 835
6. 904
7. 817
8. 1,202
9. 1,515
10. 1,400

Page 39
1. 64
2. 265
3. 307
4. 121
5. 935
6. 1,011
7. 812
8. 142
9. 1,242
10. 299

MANE STREET

Page 40
1.
$$\begin{array}{r} 1 \\ 27 \\ +\ 28 \\ \hline 55 \end{array}$$
2.
$$\begin{array}{r} 195 \\ +\ 55 \\ \hline 250 \end{array}$$
3.
$$\begin{array}{r} 1\ 1 \\ 242 \\ +\ 179 \\ \hline 421 \end{array}$$

Page 41
1. 11
2. 2
3. 30
4. 28
5. 34
6. 45
7. 53
8. 1
9. 76
10. 81

Page 42

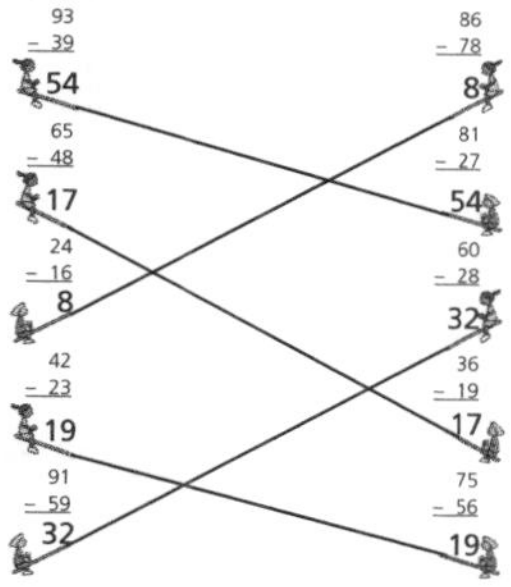

93 − 39 = 54
86 − 78 = 8
65 − 48 = 17
81 − 27 = 54
24 − 16 = 8
60 − 28 = 32
42 − 23 = 19
36 − 19 = 17
91 − 59 = 32
75 − 56 = 19

Page 43
1. 36
2. 18
3. 36
4. 27
5. 36
6. 9
7. 45
8. 54
9. 27
10. 54

Page 44
1. 134
2. 422
3. 715
4. 300
5. 616
6. 541
7. 254
8. 827
9. 111
10. 753

Page 45
1. 519
2. 246
3. 618
4. 157
5. 284
6. 783
7. 365
8. 918
9. 559
10. 451

Page 46

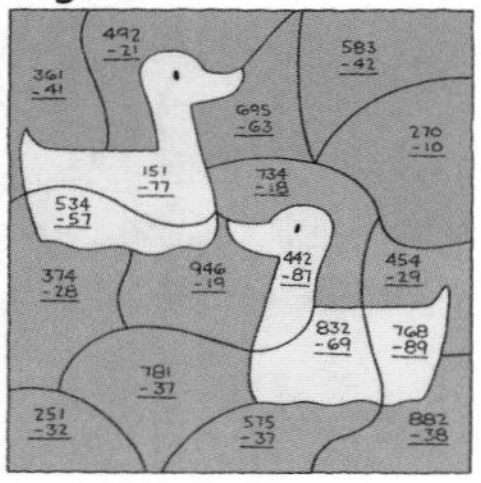

Page 47
1. 342
2. 205
3. 440
4. 312
5. 523
6. 134
7. 158
8. 52
9. 301
10. 540

Page 48
1. 114
2. 226
3. 439
4. 263
5. 5
6. 447
7. 305
8. 133
9. 268
10. 91

Page 49
1. 225 − 150 = 75
2. 225 − 75 = 150
3. 365 − 25 = 340

Page 50
1. 153 − 87 = 66
2. 591 − 423 = 168
3. 280 − 194 = 86

Page 51
1. 92
2. 30
3. 45
4. 117
5. 28
6. 19
7. 40
8. 7
9. 26
10. 110

Page 52

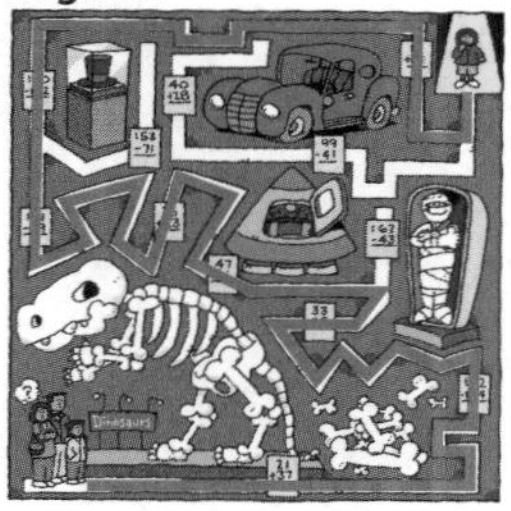

Page 53
1. 10 − 3 = 7; 10 − 7 = 3
2. 22 − 14 = 8; 22 − 8 = 14
3. 46 − 35 = 11; 46 − 11 = 35
4. 87 − 82 = 5; 87 − 5 = 82
5. 101 − 40 = 61; 101 − 61 = 40

Page 54
1. 2 + 4 = 6; 4 + 2 = 6
2. 8 + 9 = 17; 9 + 8 = 17
3. 215 + 40 = 255; 40 + 215 = 255
4. 58 + 3 = 61; 3 + 58 = 61
5. 27 + 75 = 102; 75 + 27 = 102

Page 55

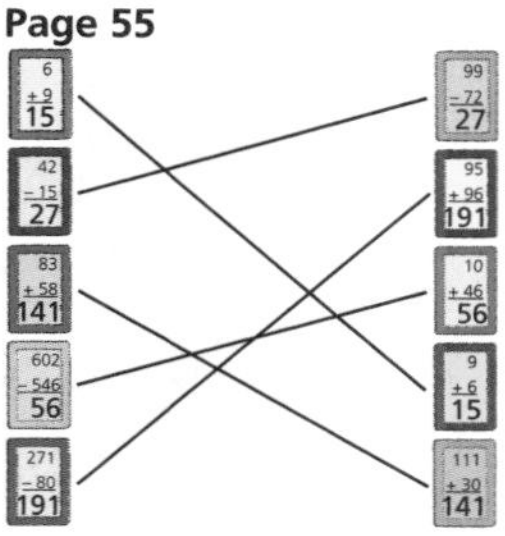

6 + 9 = 15
42 − 15 = 27
83 + 58 = 141
602 − 546 = 56
271 − 80 = 191
99 − 72 = 27
95 + 96 = 191
10 + 46 = 56
9 + 6 = 15
111 + 30 = 141

Page 56
1. 263 + 718 = 981
2. 520 − 440 = 80
3. 2 + 5 + 3 = 10

Yes, they have enough tickets.

Page 57
1. 4 + 4 = 8
2. 3 + 3 + 3 + 3 = 12
3. 5 + 5 + 5 = 15
4. 2 + 2 + 2 + 2 = 8
5. 1 + 1 + 1 + 1 + 1 = 5
6. 6 + 6 + 6 = 18
7. 4 + 4 + 4 + 4 + 4 = 20
8. 5 + 5 + 5 + 5 = 20
9. 2 + 2 + 2 + 2 + 2 + 2 = 12
10. 3+3+3+3+3+3+3=21

Page 58

2. 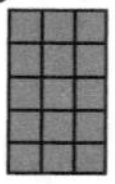 15

3. 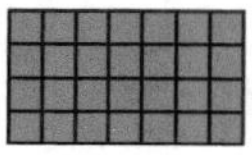 28

4. 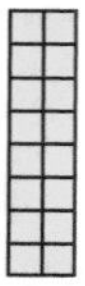 16

5. 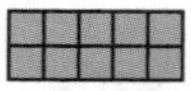 10

6. 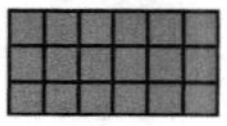 18

7. 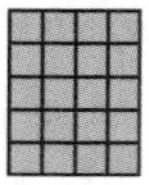 20

8. 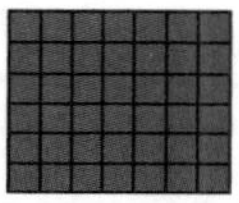 42

9. 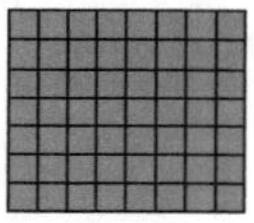 56

10. 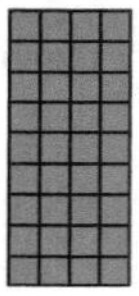 36

Page 59
1. 4 − 2 − 2 = 0; 4 ÷ 2 = 2
2. 10 − 5 − 5 = 0; 10 ÷ 5 = 2
3. 12 − 4 − 4 − 4 = 0; 12 ÷ 4 = 3
4. 6 − 3 − 3 = 0; 6 ÷ 3 = 2
5. 8 − 4 − 4 = 0; 8 ÷ 4 = 2
6. 15 − 5 − 5 − 5 = 0; 15 ÷ 5 = 3
7. 20 − 5 − 5 − 5 − 5 = 0; 20 ÷ 5 = 4
8. 14 − 2 − 2 − 2 − 2 − 2 − 2 − 2 = 0; 14 ÷ 2 = 7
9. 16 − 4 − 4 − 4 − 4 = 0; 16 ÷ 4 = 4
10. 20 − 10 − 10 = 0; 20 ÷ 10 = 2

Page 60
2. draw two bunches with six balloons each; 6
3. draw four bunches with two balloons each; 2
4. draw five bunches with three balloons each; 3
5. draw four bunches with five balloons each; 5
6. draw six bunches with five balloons each; 5
7. draw three bunches with six balloons each; 6
8. draw three bunches with three balloons each; 3
9. draw four bunches with four balloons each; 4
10. draw five bunches with two balloons each; 2

Page 61
1. 6 + 6 + 6 + 6 = 24; 6 x 4 = 24
2. 3 + 3 + 3 + 3 + 3 = 15; 3 x 5 = 15
3. 2 + 2 + 2 + 2 = 8; 2 x 4 = 8

Page 62
1. 30 − 5 − 5 − 5 − 5 − 5 − 5 = 0; 6; 30 ÷ 5 = 6
2. 12 − 6 − 6 = 0; 2; 12 ÷ 6 = 2
3. 60 − 10 − 10 − 10 − 10 − 10 − 10 = 0; 6; 60 ÷ 10 = 6

Page 63

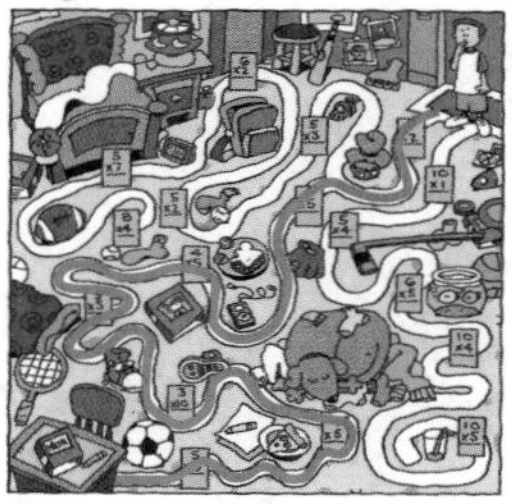

Page 64
2. color one section
3. color one section
4. color two sections
5. color three sections
6. color two sections
7. color four sections
8. color three sections
9. color five sections
10. color one section

Page 65
1. $\frac{1}{3}$
2. $\frac{6}{8}$
3. $\frac{4}{5}$
4. $\frac{2}{4}$
5. $\frac{7}{10}$
6. $\frac{1}{2}$
7. $\frac{3}{6}$
8. $\frac{2}{7}$
9. $\frac{4}{10}$
10. $\frac{9}{9}$

Page 66
1. $\frac{2}{4} < \frac{3}{4}$
2. $\frac{2}{3} > \frac{1}{3}$
3. $\frac{4}{5} > \frac{2}{5}$
4. $\frac{1}{6} < \frac{3}{6}$
5. $\frac{4}{4} > \frac{1}{4}$
6. $\frac{5}{5} = \frac{3}{3}$
7. $\frac{5}{7} > \frac{3}{7}$
8. $\frac{1}{2} < \frac{2}{2}$
9. $\frac{1}{2} = \frac{2}{4}$
10. $\frac{4}{6} > \frac{1}{3}$

Page 67

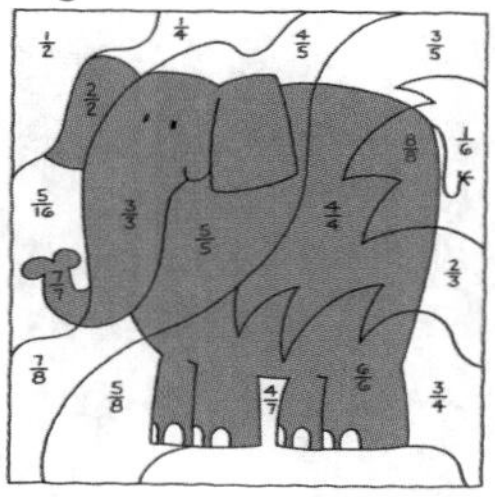

Page 68
1. 3¢
2. 10¢
3. 40¢
4. 75¢
5. 25¢
6. 54¢
7. 42¢
8. 61¢
9. $1.05
10. $1.11

Page 69
1. $2.00
2. $15.00
3. $43.00
4. $5.25
5. $10.40
6. $1.79
7. $45.25
8. $30.30
9. $3.00
10. $26.05

Page 70

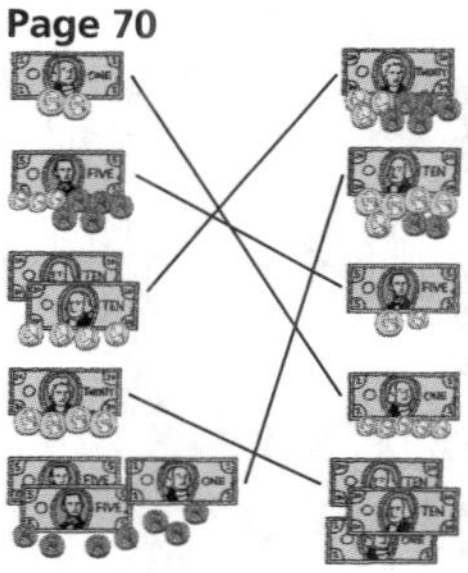

Page 71
1. circle three quarters, two dimes, and four pennies
2. circle three $1 bills, two dimes, and one nickel
3. circle $10 bill, one $5 bill, one quarter, and nickel
4. circle two $20 bills, one $10 bill, and two $1 bills
5. circle $5 bill, three $1 bills, one quarter, four dimes, and one nickel
6. circle $10 bill, one $1 bill, three quarters, and one dime
7. circle one $20 bill, four $1 bills, two quarters, one dime, and seven pennies
8. circle $10 bill, four $1 bills, three quarters, and three dimes

Page 72
2. draw one nickel
3. draw $1 bill
4. draw $5 bill and three pennies
5. draw $5 bill, $1 bill, and one dime
6. draw $20 bill and $10 bill
7. draw $10 bill, two $1 bills, and two pennies
8. draw $5 bill, three $1 bills, and one quarter
9. draw two $1 bills
10. draw $5 bill, four $1 bills, and two dimes

Page 73

Page 74
1. 25
    25
    25
    + 5
    80¢
    no
2. 39
    + 39
    78¢
3. one

Page 75

Page 76
1. 12:00
2. 6:30
3. 9:00
4. 11:00
5. 4:30
6. 2:00
7. 7:30
8. 3:30
9. 1:00
10. 10:30

Page 77
2. 1
3. 2, 30
4. 30
5. 3
6. 1, 30
7. 3, 30
8. 2
9. 4
10. 5, 30

Page 78

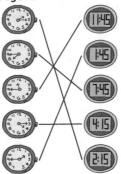

Page 79
1. 8:15
2. 9:45
3. 3:15
4. 6:45
5. 12:15
6. 5:15
7. 10:45
8. 2:45
9. 1:15
10. 11:45

Page 80
2. 45
3. 45
4. 1, 45
5. 15
6. 2
7. 2, 45
8. 2, 15
9. 3, 15
10. 45

Page 81
1. 2 hours
2. 12:00
3. 45 minutes

Page 82

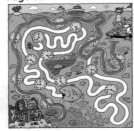

Page 83
1. 2
2. 4
3. 3
4. 6
5. 5

Page 84
1. 1
2. 5
3. 2
4. 6
5. 7

Page 85
1. 12
2. 9
3. 18
4. 16
5. 19

Page 86

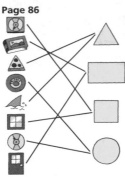

Page 87
1. triangle, 3
2. square, 4
3. rectangle, 4
4. circle, 0
5. triangle, 3
6. rectangle, 4

Page 88

Page 89

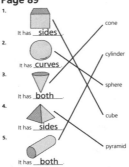

1. It has __sides__   cone
2. It has __curves__   cylinder
3. It has __both__   sphere
4. It has __sides__   cube
5. It has __both__   pyramid

Page 90
1. color blue square
2. color yellow circle, yellow circle, yellow circle
3. color brown diamond
4. color orange triangle
5. color gray square, green rectangle
6. color brown rectangle, blue triangle
7. color pink circle, yellow diamond
8. color gray rectangle, green rectangle, gray rectangle
9. color blue diamond, purple triangle, blue square
10. color green triangle, green triangle

Page 91
1. draw and color yellow circle, brown square
2. draw and color blue square
3. draw and color brown rectangle, red rectangle, brown rectangle, red rectangle
4. draw and color pink diamond, orange square
5. draw and color green rectangle, yellow rectangle, gray triangle
6. draw and color red square, purple triangle, brown circle, red square
7. draw and color blue triangle, pink rectangle
8. draw and color purple diamond, brown circle
9. draw and color green triangle, pink rectangle, green square
10. draw and color blue circle, orange circle, purple circle, gray circle

Page 92
1. 6
2. 14
3. 9
4. 16
5. 25
6. 43
7. 39
8. 60
9. 27
10. 100

Page 93
1. 10, 15
2. daisies, roses
3. 5